What's for lunch?

Potatoes

This edition 2003

Franklin Watts
96 Leonard Street
London
EC2A 4XD

Franklin Watts Australia
45-51 Huntley Street
Alexandria
NSW 2015

Editor: Samantha Armstrong
Series Designer: Kirstie Billingham
Designer: Kelly Flynn
Consultant: The Potato Marketing Board
Reading Consultant: Prue Goodwin, Reading and Language
Information Centre, Reading

A CIP catalogue record for this book is available from the British Library
Dewey Decimal Classification Number 633

ISBN: 0 7496 4942 9

Printed in Hong Kong, China

What's for lunch?

Potatoes

Claire Llewellyn

W

FRANKLIN WATTS
LONDON • SYDNEY

Today we are having potatoes for lunch.
Potatoes are a **vegetable**.
They contain **vitamins**, **fibre** and **starch**.
They give us **energy**.

Potatoes are grown all over the world.
There are many different kinds of potato.

They can be large or small,
red, brown or white.

Potatoes grow on plants. Most plants grow from a seed, but potato plants grow from another potato. In spring, farmers plant rows and rows of potatoes.

On every potato
there are little marks called **eyes**.
When the potato is planted,
shoots grow from the eyes.

After a few weeks, one of the shoots
grows towards the light
and bursts through the soil.
Under the ground,
the plant is growing **roots** and **stems**.

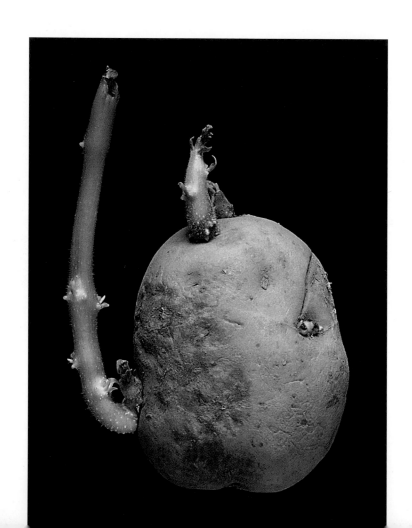

The fields are soon full of low,
bushy potato plants.
Meanwhile under the ground tiny
swellings called **tubers** grow on the stems.
These become the potatoes that we eat.

Farmers water the plants
and spray them with **chemicals**
to protect them from
pests and disease.
The potatoes grow underground,
in the dark.
If any light gets on
the potatoes, they will
turn green and
be bad to eat.

17

In autumn the leaves on the plants **wither**.
Under the ground the potatoes
are ready for **harvesting**.
A **potato harvester** digs up the potatoes
and shakes off the stones and soil as well.

The potatoes are packed into sacks
and stored in a cool, dark place.
Some are saved for planting next spring.

20

Most of the potatoes are sold to shops, markets and supermarkets where you can buy them to cook at home.
Others are sold to restaurants and hotels.

The potatoes are washed and sorted
into different sizes before they are eaten.
Any damaged or green ones are removed.

Potatoes are used in many different ways.
Some are made into crisps.
Different flavourings are added
to give them special tastes.

Potatoes can be sliced up
and fried to make chips.
Potatoes contain a lot of **starch**.
Starch is smooth and sticky
and is used to make ice-cream.

Potatoes are eaten
all over the world
in all kinds of ways.

They can be dipped
into sauces,
eaten with curry
and made into croquettes.
Potatoes are filling and good for you.

Glossary

chemical   something that farmers use on their plants to keep them healthy and strong

disease   something that attacks plants

energy   the strength to work and play

eyes   the part of a potato from which the shoots grow

fibre   something found in certain foods which helps us to digest the food we eat

pest   an insect that attacks plants

potato harvester   a machine that pulls up the potato plant and shakes off the soil

roots   the part of a plant that grows underground and takes moisture and goodness from the soil

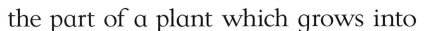

seed	the part of a plant which grows into a new plant
starch	a smooth, sticky substance found in potatoes. It is used in ice-cream.
stem	the underground part of the potato plant that the tubers grow on
tuber	an underground stem that swells into a vegetable
vegetable	a plant grown for the parts that can be eaten
vitamin	something that is found in fresh fruit and vegetables that keeps the body healthy
wither	to dry up and die

Index

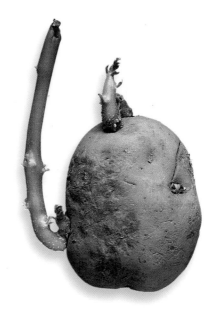

Picture credits: Barrie Watts 12, 13, 15, 18; Holt Studios International 9, 14, 16, 17, 19 (all Nigel Cattlin), 20, 21, 23 (all Richard Anthony); Image Bank 24 (Ross Horowitz); Reed Farmers Publishing Picture Library 10-11; Tayto Ltd. 25; Zefa 22; Steve Shott cover; All other photographs Tim Ridley, Wells Street Studios, London.
With thanks to Redmond and Roxanne Carney.